ORIGINAL SOUNDTRACK

ORIGINAL SOUNDTRACK
BY
DOMINIC J P NELSON-ASHLEY

For further information
on Dominic JP Nelson-Ashley,
please visit
www.djpnelsonashley.com
www.blackwords.org

First published 2018 by Ek Zuban
c/o 52 Carlow Street
Middlesbrough
TS1 4SD
United Kingdom
www.ekzuban.org.co.uk

EK ZUBAN
ISBN: 978-0-9935006-1-9
Copyright © Dominic JP Nelson-Ashley.
Edited by Bob Beagrie
Cover image by Kev Howard
Cover design by Robyn Rowan Beagrie

Dedicated to WD.

INTRO

Is it an autobiography? Is it a self-help book?
Is it Music Journalism? Is it a collection of Spoken word /
poetry pieces for live performance? Is it homework?

It is all of those things and neither at the same time.
It's for Young Adults
(not surprising as I have 2 teenagers)

because –

The only thing left on my bucket list is to see
The Specials.

There was a time when as a young black boy
living in the U.K, all I wanted to do was survive.

This took me 50 years to live and 2 weeks to write.

CONTENTS

Money
Wanna Be Starting Somethin'?

THE END: REASONS TO BE CHEERFUL 123?
Black Mafiosa Three
Bruce Lee
All hail the Chief
Duke Road Reprise
The Last Word
Once in a lifetime (Bonus Track)

HEADSPACE

BACK OF MY HEAD

On the left, in the grey corner
a local lad, local born and bred,
no nickname required (cos everybody knows him) and
in the black brown and tanned corner...

Moi

There is a reason I sound like a boxing announcer: I attack life.
pre emotive strikes, show no cracks, no weakness.

I don't fear the knockouts.
I fear the concussion, the dizziness, the lack of focus caused by
sly media rabbit punches to the back of the head.

A roundhouse kick when I thought we were playing chess.

You laugh, I sigh.
You gasp at the realisation at what this is.
You can exhale if you want to.
Many do not get that luxury. So I lean on the ropes,
tuck in to take some blows,
ready for those

who've got plenty of spare twine for a lynching
or making shoelaces.

Love me like Cassius? or only when he was
Ali? Mumbling, bedridden and lost his potency.

I am TOO LOUD you say? Somewhere
between a Rock Star and Butlin's Bluecoat.

We are cracking skulls tonight? No. Cracking jokes.

But on stage under the lights I am always thinking
how many I've known, lost to police choke holds.

Hold onto that thought whilst I hit you back.
I don't have time to enunciate, try and placate, find
some middle ground
    when I taste the canvas.

Let's get ready to rumble?
You've already given me the nickname 'trouble' - so
whatever happens next,
I am going to have to take you with me.

    Down
            with no holds barred
                    til you are asphyxiated

So that you learn
    we all breathe
                    the
                            same
                                    air.

The Bell rings: Round one.
Can you count to ten?

Think about it as I hit you with a mix
    of verboera, rhythmitsu, poetikan

How can I lose?
I have trained, whether I wanted to or not.

DUKE ROAD 1976

Nigel Bony has a big Afro, sprints faster than anybody,
walks on tip-toes,
fixes his feet in imaginary blocks,
beats the record around the playground.

Eric is 2nd.
We have a boy who reckons he's the new Alberto Juantorena
(The Cuban 400m 800m Olympic Champion).
I am only the 4th fastest.

We have a South American boy join our class called Fernando.
He talks with an accent and dialect that isn't local: Chiswick West
London English, African, Caribbean or Irish.

We tease Fernando with the Abba song. Its number one in the
charts and fourth biggest seller of the year. He smiles.
He's never heard it.

He's Brazilian but he's not as good at football as me.
20 a side, 3 goalies each and I still score.

Two boys join from Nigeria.
They buy 90% of the raffle tickets but only win a tenth of the
prizes.

Duke Road, Chiswick is its own self-contained world.
Two schools at the bottom.
My school: St Mary's Catholic Primary on the right. Hogarth C of E
on the left.
A Sweetshop a quarter of the way up.

Half way up, an Indian-owned convenience store, opposite my
house.

When mum's on a late shift, Me and my brother stay at Mrs
Gallagher's after school. the sweet natured old Swiss lady
who never lost her accent. She would make us precisely cut
egg sandwiches with butter and soft white bread.

Mum is half scowling half laughing. I've invited the whole class
back to mine again. Terence, William, Leo, everybody. Juice
and biscuits all round, in the garden.

I am the Sheriff of Nottingham in the School play. I have a tin
foil sword.

Leo is Robin Hood.

On the weekend, Dad fixes our dark green Ford Corsair with a
Ford Cortina engine. The front is curved. From the side,
it looked like a jet nose of Concorde.

Michael, the adopted Chinese boy from the other side of the
street, has a Raleigh Grifter with chunky wheels. It feels like a
motor bike. The gear changer is part of the handle grips, twist
to go faster. It's a real motor bike when we peg a piece of
paper to the back wheel, for the revved up sound.

It's hot.
We all wear shorts.
We are 10.
Nigel's mum loves Calypso.
William's dad loves the horses.

Leo loves acting up.
I write stories. Science Fiction ones.
Dad deciphers my scrawl and gets them typed up.
I proudly show my teacher.

It won't be long before the class take our first Holy Communion -
girls in white dresses, boys in grey shorts, red ties, white shirts.
We'll march two by two, taking up the width of the pavement,
moving up the length of the road to the top - the end of our known
universe, the catholic church.

It is hot.
It is 1976.
I am happy.

PRAYER (TRILOGY PART 1)

Hi God,

got a minute?

First of all, thanks for the Melanin. It really suits me.
I know it must be in short supply cos you've missed out the
soles of my feet.

Are these your words you've scribbled over me? Am I your
unfinished diary?

Did you get over-enthusiastic with calligraphy,
doodle in densely joined-up writing -
then the rain made the ink run and the sun baked it dry?

That's happened to my homework too.

Is that your signature on my palm?
A Gypsy at the fayre tried to read it. She was crap.
                            I didn't get my money back.

Hi God,

If you're not too busy, can we have a chat?
I know you're supposed to be almighty,
all-powerful and all that,
but I think you messed up.

You've been running out of paint at The People Factory again,
haven't you?

16

I appreciate you giving me the last few drops,
cos people without it
                        chase me,
keep trying to grab a piece of me
as if
     I am
the last black leather coat in the January sales.

Or
follow me around
like I'm one of your deities.
          I'm only six.
I don't think I'm ready for that kind of responsibility yet.

Hi God,

You know this Melanin thing?
I think a lack of it can affect people's brains.
Some of those Nazis outside shave off all their hair,
          burn red in the sun trying to get a tan
and cover their skin in pictures that have spelling mistakes.

Hi God,

Are you listening?
I've got a few questions cos I'm really not getting it.
Is it like my teacher said:
Blank paper is for doodling and working things out?

Hi God,

I think I've got it sussed now.

You skimped on your homework, didn't you?
Mum said that's not allowed.
You didn't give them a story.
After church, you had a lazy Sunday.
You took the weekend off.

That's why they paint Swastikas on their bodies,
make up their own naughty tattoos.

Did you run out of plots?
When kids at my school get behind, they have to catch up
in the Easter Holidays.
Is that what you're going to do?

Hi God,

Dad says the landline is really really expensive,
so if I call somebody I should get them to call back.
It's your turn to call next.
Bye.

YOUTH

ST MARK'S

I

So you reckon you're tough? So you think you're hard?
I'm from Hounslow West London.
School of hard knocks,
St. Marks.

By the bus station, 1977
Concrete playground and rock solid hearts.
Three-lane carriageway, slow lane education.
8 til 4. That's us.

So you think you're tough? So you reckon you're hard?
I'm from Hounslow West London,
run down Secondary,
St. Marks.

We got
Dave Ranalli, David Ions, Arturo Travagli.
We got
a melting pot of skin colours, flared trousers and theatre lovers
strutting about wearing
round-topped wooden-soled beetle crushers.

We got
Lance and the sport-obsessed long-limbed Afro boys.
We got
Mark Delph and Bobby Verma in the brief case squad.
Super smart, you know.

We got kids riding bareback in the toilets.
We got a 12-year-old boy - broke into the Headmaster's office,
got drunk on whisky then stole a bus. A bus!
We got a kid who got run over, brushed it off and said:
huh, I am still going in for the knowledge.'
And we got dreams. We all got dreams.

So you reckon you're tough? So you think you're hard?
I'm from Hounslow West London.
School of harsh truths,
St. Marks.

II

St. Marks?
Never heard of us?
Rule number one: What goes on in school, stays in school.
Rule number two:
don't get caught fighting,
in between the quick-fire break-time gobbling and fingering
do not,
under any circumstances,
get caught,
fighting.

A swing with the left, a lean in with the right.
What's that?
A raw undefined attempt at an uppercut.
Oh really?

When the P.E teacher catches boys punching,

He's got a single solution in his armoury.
No other options at the refectory table –
No detention, no lines, no expelling, no explanation,
no letter home.

He barks:
Roll up, roll up, roll up.
Everybody line up at the gym door.
Have your one penny entrance fee ready.
Get your bum sat around the mat.
Two mop-haired warriors going toe to toe.
No grappling, no holding, no mouth-guards, no refunds.

Each boxer gives a barrage of blows with gloves
bigger than their heads.
The shortest the most vicious with wild swings.
A quick victory.
Early stoppage.
TKO.
Done.

I hear:
Soft-bellied juveniles these days can't take a punch.
A southpaw from life?
They take a ten count, give up.
So I've got to ask:
How many rounds can you go?

We got
Alumni bus drivers, celebrities and stars you don't know.
We had dreams. We all had dreams.
For every Declan McManus there is an Elvis Costello.

We had dreams. We all had dreams.

So you think you're tough? So you reckon you're hard?
I'm from Hounslow West London.
School of real life,
I represent St. Marks.

KARA

The first chat up line of mine that ever worked.
'Do you like The Specials?'

Along with the other 2-Tone label groups, with their mix
of black and white, Caribbean Ska off-beat rhythms
and British Punk energy were the soundtrack
to my teenage life.

The first music that spoke to me directly.

Kara was 14 and looked like the younger sister
of Pauline Black from The Selecter.

Kara: Light black skin, frizzy black hair and Rara skirt
(or was it jeans?)
She was on her way left, to the Children's home
she was living at.
I suggested we take a right and go to where
I was going on that Monday night.
The Youth Club.

I was the only Afro-Caribbean teenager in the area,
she was the first
black teenage girl in the area I'd seen.
I felt like God had looked upon

my plight and dropped this creature
of loveliness into my world.

By the time we reached the Youth Club door. we were holding
hands and officially going out.

Monday night:
Kissing, Billiards, Table Tennis and The Specials live on TV.
Specials Live on the Telly - the bosses of the 2-Tone movement.
the black and white group with aggressive Ska off-beats,

doing *Skinhead Symphony*: a medley of *Long shot kick de bucket,
Liquidator* and *Skinhead moonstomp.*

Other kids had bad choices:
(1) New Wave - the hangover from punk, cardboard cut outs
with plodding root-note basslines. (2) Metal bands with
interchangeable screaming long-haired lead singers.

(3) John Lennon.

I had:
2-Tone.The Specials:
Too much too young, Message to Rudy, Ghost town –
all echoed my moods and moodswings.

The Selecter: *3 Minute Hero, On My Radio, Too Much Pressure* -
I'd bop my head along to as if I was wearing invisible headphones.

Madness had the dance-floor filling instrumental,
One Step Beyond, clever wordplay with *My Girl.*
Kids thinking they're cool cos they've memorised all the words
to *Baggy Trousers* and shout along.

Ranking Roger's Reggae toasting vocals
were for my ears only.
Hit after hit after hit.

It made me walk tall. Made me feel knowledgeable
because I had the originals (out of my dad's record box).
I knew where this music came from.
There was a history to it I was already linked to.

What did other kids have?
Punk was dead, it was about anarchy, breaking things,
but offered no solutions.
Sid was in rehab and everybody knew he couldn't play bass.

Metal was just shouting for no apparent reason by people
who loved home-brew and denim too much.
Ska had proper lyrics with a purpose.
Ghost town, Rat Race.

2-Tone fired up me up, working for unity
and fighting the system.
There was no turning back with the Beat's ode
to the evils of Thatcherism,
in my record collection.

All things come to an end. Bands left 2-Tone.
The Specials split up.
What happened to me and Kara?
It lasted about 2 sweet weeks.

GHOSTS

She's got pale blue eyes with a hint of grey,
fog rolling off an Irish mountain or a dewy winter morning.

Claire has blue eyes,
and a jumper that, to my recollection in the night,
is tight enough to make me think about
combing my knotted Afro and buying some aftershave.

What does that mean?

She has flat black hair that lies across her shoulders
and her eyes widen when I look at her.
What does that mean?

It's my birthday.
a present:
5-inch long Mars Bar in Christmas wrapping
chocolate outside
caramel soft toffee inside.

What does that mean?

She makes my charcoal-coloured cheeks hot.
What does that mean?

She sits next to me in Geography:
studying mountains, tectonic plates -
how they rub up against each other, disrupt, grate and slide.

History:
studying Ancient civilisations -
how they rub up against each other, disrupt, grate and slide.

Biology:
Boobs, Fallopian tubes.

Is it alright if I stay behind, sir?
Extra curricular?
Until this feeling subsides.

Geography again,
with a wafer thin gap between us, measured
to several decimal places.
She squeezes my inner thigh.

What does that mean?

Friday. Disco
Darkness
Tunes
Uptempo ones to throw our bodies around to.
She ignores them.

What does that mean?

I know the DJ
'Ghosts'
The sound of Japan:
Slow,
Analog flutes,
Reverberated glockenspiels.

Off-key mallets.

We have
Dry ice and space.
She grabs my bum, crushes me into her navy blue jumpsuit.
I think I know what this means.

Drunken eager kisses long after the song ends.

Just when I thought I was winning and my chance came to be king.

My African father's bass voice, louder than the disco speakers.
'What is dis report? Your work is slipping.'
'Let us look at de list of jobs: Lawyer? Doctor? Engineer?'
'Gigolo is not there.'
'End dis inter-cultural non-academic foolishness.'
'Casanova is not on de curriculum, eh eh.'

I see her picture, older.
first thing that gets me
before the clothes, Gaelic tin whistles and the Guinness pints,
is the hint of school foggy morning misty blue eyes.

YOU COULD DO SO MUCH BETTER

Tell us a secret? demanded the girls,
working in a floating point pincer movement
that corralled me into a corner by the Dining Hall wall.

Tell us all your secrets, they said
wafting a haze of Apple-blossom truth serum
they had squirted on their necks and wrists.

I read Science Fiction: Stuff about different dimensions,
where crazy things happen.

In the future we'll have phones without wires,
transmitting thoughts through air.

We'll have implants so we can understand all
the languages of this earth
(so we won't have to learn French).

We'll have music made of ones and zeroes.
We will have the ability to travel through time and space,
beyond our solar system.

Anything else?
I code mainframe computers in my spare time.
Boring, they said.

Who do you fancy? Who's in your top three?
Don't be shy.
You say them, we'll write them down.

Kick off with Jackie, aye? That's a no-brainer.
She's on everybody's list.
The Queen of the Hockey team, Netball too.
Betchya she could beat half the boys in a race.

In the safety of the whirring, heavily-fanned
computer suite, which smelt of dry dust,
my tongue-tied self, toiled away
in front of luminous green-lit VDUs
with handfuls of floppy disks,
thinking

ONE DAY
there'll be cyborgs that move faster than Jackie-
but a better curvature than her legs - in this world,
I doubt it.

ZOOM:
Mini skirt, sexy earlobes, socks around her ankles,
burgundy jumper, yellow blouse,
short hair, boundless energy.
Jackie ran up at me faster than any robot I could imagine.

I heard you got off with a girl outside the top ten? Is that true?
I heard you got off with a girl outside the top ten?
When did that happen?

I heard you got off with a girl outside the top ten?
Which space-time continuum was that in?

Error Report.

She gave me a look
my logic could not decipher.
A thought process I was too slow to catch.

She said to me:
'D, You could do so much better.'
Then she spun around, laughing
teleporting the length of the corridor in between
blinks of my eyes.

Gone.

Somewhere in a galaxy far far away, with hover cars
and babel fish,
there is a version of me
that went out with the Queen of the Hockey team
for a summer, who I serenaded with digital beats.

NOAH'S ARK

We have one of everything here, but no beggars.
We have one of everything. We have all we need.
Summertime is forever.

We have:
One Punk Rocker.
One row of houses with Roman Pillars.
One boy with Christmas decorations in his bedroom all year round.

We have:
One type of weather. 10th July.
Summertime is forever.

We have a statue of Alfred, the old king
but nobody could remember what he looked like,
so we chiselled on the face of a local councillor.

Drunkards, rebels, undesirables try to climb it
every 31st December Midnight, to break the new year in.

We have: One Black family.
One half-caste lot living at the Children's home.
We have a Woolworths 'Pick and Mix'.
We have one Chinese Takeaway - Jade Palace.
Chips & curry sauce to go.

We lied:
We have 2 churches:
One Protestant, one Catholic. We don't need any more.

We have two priests:
One Priest does masses for IRA hunger striker Bobby Sands.
He'll have to leave.
The one worshipping at the heavenly breasts
of the 16-year-old Virgin Mary?

He can stay.
We have four TV channels.
We have many opportunities for you to be,
Whatever the factory up the road wants you to be.

We are at the centre.
We are in the middle of middle England.
We have problems like everybody else.
Summertime is forever.

The Punk Rocker went bald.
The Jade Palace is closing down.
We need more security around the statue.
Kids watch too much TV.
Scientists say Global Warming is real.
Summertime is forever.

KERRY WILSON

Kerry is fading in my memory.
a ghost I refuse to let go of.

I can't see his smile anymore.
I can't remember what we talked about.
I still see his wisps of yellow hair on the head
of strangers and cry when I think of him
more than two and a half lifetimes later.

He was frail, wore glasses,
inverted chest, pipe-cleaner arms,
never said much. We played chess.
I always greeted him with a smile.
King takes your bishop in five moves.
We would sit in the alcove, the sun bouncing off our glasses.

'Kerry in today? No, sorry mate, ain't seen him.'
'Hi Kerry, where you been?'
'Around.'
Queen takes your pawn in ten easy moves.

We drank soft drinks, tap water, talked about lessons.
Did we talk about the girls we fancied?
I can't remember.
My bishop takes you out in seven easy moves.

'Is Kerry in today? No. I ain't seen him.'
Anybody want a game, remember pawn moves first.
'Anybody seen Kerry?'
'Haven't you heard? Kerry's dead.'

I'd never heard of Cystic Fibrosis.
Ah, that explains the coughing and wheezing?
The skiving off A-level lessons that were drilled into our heads
as essential for our future?
And why we never saw him at the Discos
(except once, I think?)

I remember the feeling of the look his mother gave me.
'He was ill but he never wanted it to define him.
He talked about you all the time.
You were his best friend.'

Kerry is a feeling I never want to let go.
His face has disappeared.
I know he had blonde hair.
We played chess.
We loved to talk about -
About?
Checkmate.
See you in the afterlife, mate.
Because I can't remember where
the Garden of Remembrance is,
with the tree they planted for you,
so I got to honour you in my own way, OK?
I'll see you when I see you, yeah.
And we can catch up on all the things
I've done without you.
Chat about how my kid is the same age
you were when you left.
Me?
I don't play chess anymore.
Why?

I can't see the board through my tears.
And the candles I light in your name in the churches
I pass don't burn as bright as the sun in the sixth form alcove.

'Anybody seen Kerry? Kerry Wilson.
Blonde. Skinny. Kept himself to himself.
Knew who his friends were. He was right here.'

DAMAGED GOODS

We are damaged goods.
We are serene over Science notes,
listening to Culture Club
with cups of tea and cocoa
disturbed sporadically
by your aunt
who isn't actually related
but when your dad and your mum disintegrated into War
you had to have somewhere to run to.

We are damaged goods.
We race with my cycle clips, your full-length flowing skirt,
gripping handle bars with baskets for books.

We are damaged goods.
And we escape between the dialling tones,
teasing the subtext
of consequences, dreaming
of moving the platonic to the subsonic.

We are damaged goods.
And we could heal ourselves in the cracked spines,
in the essays of our worth,
in the psychology of belonging.

We are damaged goods.
Why waste our time with letters when we
live a short bike ride away?

The sizzle of the butter on toast.

You don't trust men.
'All guys will turn out like Dad.'

In Physics, you chew your nails,
stuttering nerves
electric
undercurrent.

I like a challenge.
I made you a mixtape full of re-edits –
like the thought processes we needed.
With extra sexy bass.
You thought my records were scratched.

Do you really want to hurt me?
Do you really want to make me cry?

We are damaged goods.
And there is no quick easy cycle path
to fixing what I didn't break,
what I didn't puncture, what I don't
have the instruction manual for.

I feel sick.
Are we making each other toxic?
I spin away
My bike locked up in the garage.

I listen to the arguments at home:
the breaking, the disintegrating,
wondering how far I would run to escape?
And live with an aunt who isn't my aunt.

We are out of time, out of sync.
I am ahead in the module
of prime numbers and primal feelings.
You are ahead in the observation and calculation
of survival, thermodynamics, insulation.

You are damaged goods.
I am not yet damaged enough to understand.

LAST NIGHT A DJ SAVED MY LIFE

I

Doctor Doctor: I feel like 'The Man from Atlantis'
and I've forgotten how to swim.
Doctor Doctor: Fufu, Plasas, Mackerel, Jollof rice
and my mother's love aren't enough to nourish me.

Doctor Doctor: I think I'm dying.
1.2 seconds of Antmusic (Burundi drumming)
isn't going to get me through the day.
A man cannot survive on beats alone.
Simple Minds promised me a miracle,
but I only get salvation from the bass-line,
just before the chorus kicks in.

The attack of snare drums from
'British Pop One Hit Wonders' is killing me.

Doctor Doctor: I've tried everything:
I've tasted the dark side - Iron Maiden.
Alternative medicine – Siouxse and the Banshees.
Immersion therapy – The mosh pit at a 'Damned' concert,
but nothing's working.
The roar
of the crowd
at the 'Thompson Twins' concert
kept me
sedated
for six months.

Doctor Doctor: can't you see I'm hurting, hurting?

II

It takes a nation of 50 million to hold me back,
but only a town of 15,000 to make me feel comatose.
It takes a nation of millions to hold me back,
but only a one-way ticket to a Led Zep'-infected Polytechnic
to get me hooked on troubadours fuelled
by weed and morphine.

III

1987
A packed Hammersmith Apollo.
Def Jam tour.
'Yo, bum rush the show.'
Terminator X on the decks.
I am soaked, baptised, reborn in sweat.
Public Enemy own the stage.
They have sliced up James Brown's 'Funky Drummer',
baked and caked it for me.
I digest the lyrics.
I am cured.
I testify to the healing powers of music.
Beyond 81, 82 ,83, 84, I found my new gold dream.
My screams are enshrined on wax with 3,500 others
in the opening bars of 'Countdown to Armageddon'.

TRAVELOGUE

STANDING STILL

You can jive, you can smile, you can sing, you can dance,
but you can't stand still.

You can have Latin hips and African lips,
but you can't stand still.

You can run a hundred metres in ten seconds flat,
but you can't stand still.

Win Gold in the heptathlon, beat drugged-up Olympians
but you can't stand still.

You can jump, slam dunk, kick a ball, run and score,
prance, star in panto farce, shake your arse and
with your bredren - mash up de dance,

but you can't stand still.

Because if you stop - stay planted in one spot,
stay rooted,

we have to sit down and listen,
to your opinions:

reparations, TV representations, Police brutality, Blackface,
the rise of the Far-Right, Foreign Aid destabilising Africa,

The fact that Stepin Fetchit did what he had to do
just to get by.
We can't do that.

That sounds like - a lot of expenditure of energy.
That sounds like - a lot of hard work.

THE UNSAYABLE

The N-Word
is the only one
in the dictionary
that means,
'Hey, I used to own you.'

A GENTLEMAN NEVER TELLS

She is the only woman
who can freeze my heart without killing me.
She can stop
my frenetic systolic and diastolic beats with a whisper.

Whenever we are alone and she asks if I'm good,
the answer is always 'Yes' because
around her I forget the aches and pains, the stresses,
the failures, the experiments. I forget the science.
I achieve deep tranquilly – She is my Zen.
Her bewitchment over me is scary –
until I am in her presence.

Tonight, I have methodically organised the route
of my alcohol consumption.
I have it mapped out. I am walking alone,
staggering. In my head, I can handle straight lines.
In reality, I am stumbling, bumping into lampposts that argue,
fight back. I cannot orchestrate my legs.

The last bar is busier than normal, rammed.
Riotous, metallic. She is there:
ebony dreadlocks, ivory white Lab Coat
with hints of Aramaic and hieroglyphic symbols,
holding a 90cm Yard of Ale Test tube.
I offer a liqueur to add to the mix.

One word from her and I am sober.
The sound of the crowd thins into a gossamer.

'Shall we go, walk in the same direction?'
Hypnotised, I follow.
'What's new with you?' I ask.
'New concoction with crushed leaves, pestle and mortar.'
The recipe:
Three parts funk, two parts love, ancestral blessings
and a one-drop of fire water.
The snap of her fingers
(or was it the sound of her key in her front door?)
wake me up from the trance.

We are alone, silhouetted by street lights
through the slit in the thick bedroom curtains.
She takes her brown African earrings off,
carved from Yohimbe Tree bark.

I see her sweet back. Her outline,
blending with the night. I undress.
She pulls me under the covers.
I caress her areolae. She says my name
with sweet elongated syllables,
melodically a-c-a-b, long forgotten magic
that calms the spirit within me.

We sleep. I realise we are the same.
In the morning she asks if I have to go?
I curse my organisational skills.
'Around the world Pre-booked flights is a bitch.'

I call her from a red phone box planted
in the middle of the Sahara Desert.
My feet sinking in the sand-dunes.

Our conversation is stilted.
It sounds as if she is hiding her voice from someone.
I imagine he is a monster crushing her verve.

Years later I see her again,
sitting opposite me on a train.
We have identical black leather jackets.
I'm with someone else. She is alone.
The train does not feel as if it is moving.
She gives me her number.
I promise I'll call.

She is wearing the earrings I bought her:
Ones carved from blue stardust plucked
from the depths of a volcano,
caged in golden chambers forged
over millions of years that resonates
at our fundamental frequency.

I see her at a crowded party. I say 'How are you?
'Good.'
I'm at the piano. I play it safe, riffing in A minor.
She lays her hand on my shoulder.
I want to say:

We have everything and nothing.
We are trying to get to the same place
in different directions. We are the same:
two lost souls, experimenting,
searching for peace using whatever spells,
whatever magic we have at our disposal.

We have moments of seeing the future –
but only with one eye open, so it looks
as if it's only half written.

We need more than sweet extended moments of salvation.
Neither of us ever wants to feel alone.

I want to say:
The thought of you kept me grounded.
I've written songs for you
you've never heard.

This un-nameable thing that we have? This thing we had:
Lovers, friends, soul-mates?
My organised mind has a Venn diagram for that.

I want to say all that and more.
But all I say is 'Nice earrings'
because a gentleman never tells.

GENTLEMAN REPRISE

My right hand hovers over Edominant7
(It's got a Gsharp in it, for those who don't know),
ready to modulate, ready to end this,
ready to close the piano lid for the last time.

I tell her I've developed. I have other skills.
I want to say:
With the pen on paper, she infuses all my heroines.
There is a fraction of her in every one of them that I write.
I hear her voice in my head.

'This thing we had? You mean this thing we have.'
'We are multi-faceted beings.'

Her palms touch mine. The wooden
bracelets on her wrist, carved from the Yohimbe Tree,
are working hard, suppressing my overthinking,
destroying my complex flow charts
with her natural remedies.

This thing we had? You mean this thing we have.
She opens her mouth.
'We are multi-faceted beings', she says.
'With two eyes we can see the future.'

My Zen Mistress has many skills. Her kisses
can touch every part of me. She can also read minds.

WHY? (TRILOGY PART 2)

I

Hey God, remember me? Long time no see.
Why aren't I in love?
I have measured the nutritional value of her kisses.
Her skin is the colour of Red Palm oil, fried plantain and
Mexican cocoa powder.
She can feed off me for a thousand years plus one.
For her, my cream is the fountain of eternal youth.
Her moves make my molecules dance.
She whispers, I am her missing piece.
I am her BB King. She's my Queen Latifah.
Why aren't I in love?

II

We got a pickney coming.
Me? Scared? No.
Repeat.
Me? Scared? No. I can freestyle jam.
Blues licks work over everything.

The piano:
I play songs by Prince. Her favourite - Purple Rain.
Pain without trouble, trouble devoid of pain.
Simplified but she wants 'the Jazz chords' and drum solos.
Minor ninths embellished with nappies.
God, Isn't this what you want too?

III

God, remember me?
I saw a Tarot Card Reader today.
I think she's a pissed-up Travel Agent in disguise
because in-between slurs, she said I haven't
travelled far enough yet.

    Lewisham
        to Hackney
                to Ealing
                        to Southall.
                              This journey is killing me.
        Still walking,
            Still wandering,
grinding down shoe-leather, 9 til 9, in ever-decreasing circles.
Pitter-patter riddims still waiting to run?

Why aren't I in love?
Is it my work ethic?
I've doubled up on the hours, the commitment.

    East is East.
        West is West.
            North is North.
                South is South.
                And I don't know which way is up.

The band in her belly is shaping me,
twisting my bass vibrations.
They're gonna be reggae-loving babies.

They're sure to be reggae-loving babies.
Althea and Donna are uptown top-ranking names for twins.

IV

The raggamuffin
thyroid child is a ghost.

Maybe
its soul wasn't written for our tune.

I make fractured
melodies quieter than a whisper.

Coltrane teaches me:
Mixolydian Mode works over everything.

V

I fix, re-start, re-boot.
Repeat.
I fix, re-start, re-build.
Repeat.
I fix, re-start, re-glue.
Repeat.
We are moulded whole again minus one.
Broken.
Patched up.
I always leave things as I find them.
Why aren't I in love?

PENG PROVERB

Everything
in life
can be improved
by
an extra
side-order
of
fried plantain.
(and you know that's the truth.)

UNIVERSAL TRUTH (TRILOGY PART 3)

Alright luv. Listen. You are WRONG. *You're a wrong' un.*
You should not exist here. God messed up again.
You have an Afro-Cuban bum and no music at home –
vinyl or CDs. How is that possible? That defies logic.
Rest easy. Have a drink. I've got an explanation.
You're on the wrong fuckin' planet.
You should've turned left at Alpha Centauri.
You're on your way to Gamma Five, to spend years, decades
looking for my spirit, my soul in the bodies of others.
One problem luv. I'm not there. I'm here.
Transmorphing isn't possible in any universe so –
Take a short cut with a caipirinha.

Me & You? Isn't it obvious?
You were the only girl in your tiny, tiny village with a black doll.
A signal from our unborn children.
An echo of our days of future past.
You can fight it all you want.
All roads, in any parallel dimension you visit, lead back to me.

OK luv, lets do it your way. Take the long route, round trip
through the jungles of Panama, the Amazon then back to
London. You like flamenco guitars?
Dos
Cervezas
por
favor, eh.

Get the man behind the counter, in this cantina - Bolivian bar to
crank up 'Bamboleo' (by The Gypsy Kings) and let's have it out.
Pick a universe, any universe and I will show you
HOW
we are bound together.
HOW
we are intertwined.
HOW
were always destined to meet. To be.
This one? Terra Prime.
Sencillo. Easy.
Your best friend is from my 1980s Oxfordshire hometown.
I went to school with her brother. Need I say any more?

Fast forward.

Want to know about my wife? She hates the limelight.
We met in Lima, Peru,
She has no desire to change me. When my wife catches me
laughing, on our wedding day, for no apparent reason,
I tell her:
only me, my Travel Agent and God get the joke.

KIDS

I KNOW YOU (1,2,3,4) RE-EDIT

PART ONE (TWO TRIBES)

You will be a doctor my son,
he would say with fervour
or matter-of-factness that I found annoying,
then slipped into anger.
He'd say it religiously
like it was written in stone, devoid of flexibility.
It was the 11th commandment,
Along with:
I know you better than you know yourself,
I was there when you were born.

He would
accidently-on-purpose open my letters.
We have the same name and as legend has it –
added the middle name Junior because people would
pat my mother's belly and ask 'how's Junior doing today?'
He had a picture of himself on the wall entitled 'The Man Himself'
He always worked late, hated bad language
and only watched the news,
avoiding British 1970s Primetime TV classics: Alf Garnett
and the Black and White Minstrel Show.
He was a Scientific Inventor with seven white shirts.

There were very few laughs.
Drink this! he demanded of my 10-year-old self.
My mouth burned. What is it?
Whisky. Fire water. Don't drink it ever again.

Once he came home early,
we watched that first black character on Coronation Street.
Cha. that's not us. Who writes that? turn off the TV.
He fell asleep during Star Wars, snoring.
He was 45 for 5 years in a row.
*Did I ever get round to telling you about
the birds and the bees?*
It's alright dad, I'm studying A-level Biology.
He would make my blood boil.
*No need to bring home your school report I've already got it.
No need to pick up your exam results I've already got them.*

We would fight.
Once, he ripped up my 'Frankie Goes To Hollywood' T-Shirt.
I ran away from home.
I could never read him.
He hugged me unexpectedly, the day I stole money.

Hey Dad, maybe I can go off and learn
how to be a psychologist, head mechanic –
fix peoples broken souls?

*No. That job is not on the list. You will be a doctor my son.
You will be a doctor, a proper one.*

Recurring heart attacks, bedridden.
He died of prostate cancer on starched white sheets.
Tray of uneaten food on the left, oxygen tank on the right,
on an island no bigger than a football stadium
surrounded by leeching strangers, in a house
that looked like a cereal box version
of his childhood African home.

He is buried in an un-marked grave.
I said I wouldn't make the same mistakes.

PART TWO (BONKERS)

I was there when my son was born, blood sprayed,
I kissed the first gasp of air into his lungs.
I cut the cord that separated him from his mother.
She did the 9 months but I've got to do 20-years hard labour
because black boys are an endangered species.

His mum didn't want to give him my name
so I gave him one that sounds like mine
when she's had too many whiskies.
I watched his first steps, packed his bag
and watched him leave the house when we argued
hoping he'd come back.
I swore I would do whatever it took to protect him
because black boys are an endangered species.

I know all his teachers by name and nickname
Shout out to Mr Makin a.k.a the Macdaddy,
Physics teacher with the white hair, glasses and bow tie.
Who is he sitting next to? Move him.
That child's a bad influence. Move him again.
Send me exam results direct, I can't wait.
Me and Macdaddy have our own handshake.

I change my working life to protect my son from the bullshit.
I run interference, block the subliminals.
His white grandfather drops 'nigger on the woodpile'
on the beat in general conversation.
It's just a phrase, a colonial, I mean colloquial phrase.
It's just a phrase – a common, I mean commonwealth phrase.
The scratch DJ in my head has Tourette's

and cuts up Public Enemy records
ffffffff fight the power.

His mother wants to 'heal the world'
so takes our son around to play
with his KKK white grandfather again!!!!
Defence mode, I double up. Shoot them down
with The Skatalites' *Guns of Navarone*
We convene a 'clear the air' conference.

I'm a 3-minute Hero cos that's all the time I can take.
The Selecter sing in my head:
It's the same old show on my radio.
I ask God:
Is this the tax I have to pay for marrying a white woman?

In the column of debits and credits, right now
I'm gonna have to make a deduction and write you off, luv.
I triple up, tell her she's off the team:
No need for back up dancers, luv.
No need for bench warmers, luv.
You're excommunicated, luv.
It's a team of 3 – me, myself and I.
Because
Sometimes my son looks like
Barack Obama, 44th President of the Unites States of America,
Leader of the free world.
Sometimes he looks like Lewis Hamilton F1 driver,
helmet number 44.
the 1, 2, 3, 4 times world champion who beat the odds
and
sometimes he looks like he's wearing the face

of my teenage cousin who killed himself.
I know black boys are an endangered species.

Money runs through my fingers.
I pay to provide every opportunity I can.
Extra lessons, friends call him the Algebra King.
He cracks jokes I don't comprehend. I laugh anyway.

I drill into his head:
'Son, you can be anything you want to be as long as
you are the best. Love conquers fear but high grades
and a great suit conquers everything.'

My wife's got her own playlist:
Bryan Adams - Everything I do.
Paul McCartney and Stevie Wonder - Ebony and Ivory.
Black Eyed Peas - Where is the love?

My wife calls, wanting to talk:
'High blood pressure, half your face doesn't work,
you're in a wheelchair, I think you've had a stroke.
You've lost the power of speech?'
No luv, I've just been biting my tongue too hard for too long
and I can't afford an anger translator
who also knows sign language.

I persuade my son, at the 4th attempt, to take up fencing
What happened at school today, son?
'One boy says black people only eat watermelon.'
Cut him off.
'One boy says he's naturally cleverer than me!'
Cut him off.

STOP
REWIND
REPEAT
He sss-said what?
He was NATURALLY cleverer than you, regardless of effort?
CUT HIM OFF.

'I love you, dad.'
I tell him that kindness and soft words make no difference.
Because black boys are an endangered species.

My bank balance is bust.
I black out. I wake up, surrounded by broken glass.
I have developed a deep throaty menacing whisper.
'You come home with these grades, eh eh?
If your blind Caribbean great-grandma could see you now,
what would she say? 9 out of 10?
There's a whole point missing –
and that's the point.'

My son and I watch the remake of 'the Karate Kid'.
The only version you need is my success-obsessed Mr Miyagi.
Homework done? No. Xbox TV off.
Homework done? No. Xbox TV off.

I browse his internet history, analyse his Facebook profile.
His enemies are my enemies.
The parents of his enemies are my enemies.
I know which of his mates smoke weed, do Ketamine and
which only burn the midnight oil on the books.
My own birthdays don't matter.

I work 3 jobs.
I feel I am a lightweight compared to what my parents did.
Did I ever get a chance to tell you about
the birds and the bees?
'Err its ok, dad. I'm doing A-Level Biology.'

He takes his dates to a restaurant where I know the chef,
cos extra plantain improves everything.
Shout out to Amadou and Apollo at Kilimanjaro's.

My son smiles, saying I'm cool.
His friends have discovered an alternative me.
'They have your musical face as their screensaver',
he says proudly.
Soft kind words will not save you.
Black boys are an endangered species everywhere.

Are you one of those Tiger Daddies?
Applying too much pressure?
Ones who push their kids too hard?
His posh friend's father asks.
Paper Tiger? No.
My bloodline, my offspring, my scions are Lions
that cannot be caged
FYI you need to check your daughter's pages
and what she writes with her white lines.
You may be rolling in the money but she skips class,
takes MDMA and deals drugs on the Darlo college green.

I invent new riddims new rhymes
new kennings new combinations:

I am the Race-perception twister,
I am the Bad-vibe blocker,
I am the multi-career path-creator,
I am the Marriage guidance class-avoider.
Try saying that if you're drunk.

Sometimes I talk so fast my son thinks
I am channeling an Ancient African spirit.
He thinks I can do magic.
The best trick I've ever played is convincing him I'm rich
even though I wear the same clothes everyday.
I annoy him by writing down what he's thinking,
what he wants, before he says it.

'Hey dad, I'm going to be a doctor, bone-mechanic,
surgeon fixing broken bodies, maybe hearts on the side.'
How did I know? He asks,
I try not to say it
I don't want to say it
but blurt out
I know you better than you know yourself.
I was there when you were born.

PART THREE (THE CIRCLE OF LIFE)

My son's bags are packed.
He's leaving to go to Med school.

I've moved from his bottom-wiper
and piss-taker to his bank balance adjuster.

He asks for advice.
I grab him and shout in his face:
In this house, in this life, there are no tap outs, now fuck off.

Like WWF wrestling, nothing is as it appears to be.
I put him in a headlock and kiss his forehead.
Every word of this is true
but only my family know where the jokes are.

I call him back for one last hug and say:
One more thing before you go.
Phone your mum and my mum, your nan up regularly.
Treat them with love and R-E-S-P-E-C-T
cos without them, you wouldn't be here.

This is the end.
Thank you for listening - and putting the work in.

PART FOUR (WHERE IS THE LOVE?)

What of my wife?
My long suffering, international folkdance-loving wife,
who so often sits watching the drama from the side lines shouting
'You've got A-Level Physics but you can't change a lightbulb.
I've never seen you cook Jollof rice.
When are we going on holiday?'

She says she has a dream,
a dream that our children will live in a nation where
they are not judged on the colour of their skin but
by the content of their character.
I said, *You've remixed a Martin Luther King track, luv.*
Paradise sounds nice but right now I don't think I can afford the air
fare.
Has everybody else signed up for the flight?
Have you checked the small print, the terms and conditions?

She says, to the wheelchair bound, half-paralysed,
disintegrating version of me:
'D, What about unconditional love for humanity?'
'D, What about unconditional love for humanity?'
'D, What about unconditional love for humanity?'
I say, *We're both shouting for EQUALITY in our own ways.*

What of my wife, my fun-loving colour blind wife?
She wants a holiday, sweet dreams? Vegas?
Dance through the colourfields, if only
I could stop acting, in her eyes, like
the lunatics have taken over the asylum.

I jump up,
I never forget our wedding anniversary,
Twenty years, has it really been that long?
The Specials have reformed.
'Enjoy yourself', she says. 'It's later than you think.'
Black Fathers are an endangered species.

BLACK MAFIOSA

If you cross me, I will cut your head off and put it in the bin.
I will not cry.

I am not a nasty person, but I know some people who are -
and I'm going to tell them about YOU.

You leave me no choice.
You brought this upon yourself.
You don't mess with The Black Mafiosa.

You're pathetic.
You know nothing.
How much do you make?
You're not
bringing enough
moolah
to the fam.

If we weren't related, I wouldn't want to know you,
I would literally cross over to the other side of the street.

I know you're my Mum, but I don't like you - Never have, never will.
I don't think we can ever be friends.
How about unnecessary acquaintances?

When you're old, I'm not going to visit you or look after you.
You are dead weight.
So what if I'm Six?
Nobody messes with The Black Mafiosa.

BLACK MAFIOSA TWO

Why are you laughing?
I have said nothing funny.
I've put you on my list and you know what that means?
Shit gets done.
Respect the order.
Always, always, always get the details right.
I said:
I'll grab you, cut off your head
and chop your body into small pieces and put you in a bin.
I will send that bin, with you inside it,
down a hill and lose some of the pieces.
Some of the pieces WILL FALL OUT.
How can I be shady if I do it in broad daylight?
It is not my fault if other people are scared of me.
If other people fear me that's just an added bonus.
Nobody messes with the Black Mafiosa.
Shut up.
Put your hands down.
Keep them down low where I can see them
or I will end your life.
So what if I'm 15?
So what if you're proud of my school results?
I am not going to give you a 'high five' in public.
Put your hand down or I will end you.
Nobody messes with the Black Mafiosa.
Alright I'll do a fist-bump then.

My daughter is the avid
book-consumer, family house dictator
and owner of a pair of pink boxing gloves.

She looks like Sade (pronounced shah-DAY)
the Nigerian-born British RnB soul singer
(and former model) whose album Diamond Life
sold 6million copies in 1984.

My daughter has meticulous diction
as if she taught the Queen correct pronunciation.
However, the words that pour from her mouth
sound like those of a Sicilian gangster.
She loves Grime music and rap battles me with Stormzy lyrics.
She has a fantastic memory for factual recall,
sings the melody from Michael Jackson's Earth Song
out of tune to deliberately annoy me.

I love my kids equally but she gets less words
on the page because she hates me writing
or talking about her,
so if you see her - don't tell her I wrote this.
Nobody has to know.
I am currently ninth on the list of relatives she likes.
I'm happy with that. I haven't always been in the top ten.

MONEY

I said:
It is an African tradition
that you should hand over
your first pay-packet
to your parents
(as a sign of gratitude and respect).

My Firstborn, Heir to my kingdom said:
I'm only a quarter African so it doesn't apply to me.

I said:
You're really expensive to grow.
I'll take 25%.
I'll take whatever I can get.

WANNA BE STARTIN' SOMETHIN'?

You wanna be starting something?
You wanna argue?
Let's go.

ROUND ONE

Let's talk about MJ? You know who I mean:
Michael Jackson. The world's greatest entertainer.
You ask me about him and my common response is:
 I ain't got time for that. No can do.

Michael Jackson is what happens when you get
talented rich people with no squad,
no crew in their corner to shout,
'Fuck that shit. don't go there, get some sense, it ain't worth it.'

Don't get me wrong.
I love his music, saw him at a packed-out
Wembley stadium on his 'BAD' tour.

The 'Dangerous' album kept me going
through some dark times. The Jackson's 'Heartbreak Hotel'
is my jam, in my list of top ten nightclub anthems.
But –
Look at the cover of Ebony Magazine Special Edition
to mark the 25th year after the release of his Thriller LP.
(100 million sales and rising)

Ebony logo in white letters on a red background.
Top left advertising an article inside 'The Africa you don't know'

(Maybe somebody was trying to get a message to him?)

Then a full sized picture of Michael Jackson
with long straight black hair,
white skin and a straight nose.

Why Michael, why?
All artists are a little bit crazy right?
Let's tattoo Springsteen's body green,
see how that goes down?

I still remember the day I showed my son 'Off the Wall'
era photos and told him that was Michael.
He said I was lying, trying to trick him,

then asked me why did MJ do that?
Why did he change his beautiful face,
big flat African nose and all?
How am I supposed to answer that question?

All I can do for my family, my crew, my squad, my team
is protect them, toughen them up and hope they cope
with the onslaught of negativity

then pick up the pieces if they crack.
We have to counsel our children over trying
to scrub the blackness off their skin

rip out the skin-bleaching ads in all the magazines.
I am always ready to battle because Bad vibes are coming
from every direction at 1Gigabyte per second
via fibre optic cables,

24 hours a day, 7 days a week delivering gunk strong
enough that turns the world's most famous black man white.
We should all love ourselves, the way we are.

Agree?
We're all the same under the skin.
We are One Blood.

Is this a hug, a clinch?
Are you moon-walking with me?
Are you tap-dancing around the issues,

touching gloves from a distance. Lump every shade,
every creed together, tick the box marked 'politically black.'
Flatten out unique experiences?

I'm gonna have to jab you back with:
'No groups have ever needed
to be boxed in to find true solidarity.'

ROUND TWO

I'd love to live a Zen-like contemplative lifestyle.
I really would, but it doesn't work for me.
Too much battling to do.
The fight never ends.
AND
It's harder for girls,
much, much harder.
I've got to make sure my daughter's team, squad, crew
is the tightest, most rigorous, mentally toughest of them all.

She's got hassles for being black, hassles for being a woman.
Too skinny? Too fat? Got to have a thigh gap?
got to have collagen fish lips?
got to have plastic tits?

LGBT-Q-RSVP-WXY-Zee, and need a man to be complete?
When all she wants to do is
stay at home, read books
and ask if daddy's got enough money to take her horse-riding.

Nicki Minaj's artificial butt and fat jokes
from French & Saunders are not what I ordered.
I like Beyoncé but can't be dealing with her dyed blond hair.
Representation matters.

Mumbling semi-comatose rappers saying,
they don't want to be role models.
Too much pressure?
Tough. It goes with the territory.

People say I need to chill out, lighten up,
'Oh, you're just an old angry black man?'
To which I reply
YES
Still alive, still kicking.

I can't wait for another Obama
and he wasn't always the answer.
Idris Elba can't star in everything.
I've got to hit hard.

As my friend G.N.W said, 'There are no rest days.'
I fight for my friends, my kids, the people who know me.
I can't let it go to the Judges decision, cos its rigged.

Some say I can't beat it.

So before you 2-Step into Round Three,
are you in my crew, my squad, my team

or am I going to have to put on some LL Cool J,
write some words to knock you out?

THE END:
REASONS TO BE CHEERFUL 123?

BLACK MAFIOSA THREE

I

'Oh, you're writing a book sweetie, that's wonderful.
You're going to write about me obviously, aren't you?'

I can hear my cousin Elle's voice in my head,
before I've put pen to paper. A contractual obligation

I'm more than happy to comply with. She has an old-school
hip-hop soul with hippie overtones. She also has 'Boss mode'.

She can be mellow, then hit you with the legalese –
like a boss.
She can shop and have a business conference call
at the same time –
like a boss.

She's analysed the problem - and told you the solution,
before you knew there was a problem in the first place –
like a proper boss.

'I like Elle more than you,' my daughter says to my face,
not just because they have the same shoe size.

II

Elle: an integral part of my daughter's team, her squad.
She has the wisdom of ages from a path travelled,
that I can't give
and translation skills I can only step back and marvel at.

She's tall, skinny, dark-skinned with black and grey
interwoven dreadlocks
that travel all the way down her back,
and when she goes back to Africa,
they ask why she doesn't have a big African backside
(except in her favourite shabeen).

'Hey Boss Gal, why ya batty so flat, eh eh?'

'Because I walk so far so fast around the world and I
still come back.
The size of my ass got nothing to do with the shape
of my character.'

We're the same age so that means she's 49 –
and a number of months
I am not, I repeat, not allowed to say, as I've signed
a non-disclosure agreement with strict penalties attached.

And when I scratch my head, wondering why
my daughter struts around, ripping up paper and shouting
'If something's on my list then shit gets done',
Elle says:
'You know we come from a long line of organisers, thinkers,
doers, entrepreneurs, right?

We've always been more than paper-shufflers.
We dance to our own tune. We build things in any way,
shape or form we choose.'

III

Every week Elle tells me
how she micro-manages her department,
the charities she works for and the festival events she runs –
before adding that she's also micro-managing
her house renovations.
'The original contractor isn't up to the job, sweetie.'

She tells me when I'm acting too crazy.
She is the only person who can shut me up.
Once, she asked my opinion, about changing her name
to greater reflect the path she's been on?
I told her:
'You know we come from a long line of thinkers, organisers,
doers, right? We've always been more than paper-shufflers.
We dance to our own tune so we can name that rhythm,
that beat, whatever we like.'

She laughed, a mellow laugh,
telling me she'd already made up her mind - like a boss.
'Hey, You've tried to remix and repackage
my words and send them back to me, sweetie.
Make up your own.'

If ever I don't understand my daughter,

I know somebody who does.
'Ahh, what's she up to this week?' she asks.
'Oh, that's lovely. Been there, done that, worn the t-shirt,
done it in my own shoes - which I bought in bulk wholesale
and sold on at a profit. I even designed the shop logo.'

I can see the straight line between my daughter's attitude
and Elle's finely tuned 'Boss mode.'
I'm ecstatic about that.
Except -
They have each other's phone number,
speak the same language.

If they work together
I won't stand a chance.

BRUCE LEE

Me and my younger brother fight over only three things:

(1) Who is the greatest soul singer of all time?
(2) The merits (or not) of the 1980s pop group Five Star (made up from the Pearson family siblings)
(3) Who is the hardest, me or him?

Aretha Franklin is the greatest soul singer of all time.
Say a little prayer, *R-E-S-P-E-C-T*, *Rocksteady* - game over.
My brother thinks it's Otis Redding.
Sitting in the Dock of the Bay is a great piece of work.
He's in my top 5, but for me, Aretha wins every time.
Case closed.

When we were poor, my brother bought for my birthday:
a bag of oranges
a bottle of cider
Digital Underground's *The Humpty Dance* on 12inch vinyl.

It is the best present I have ever received
(narrowly beating the CD my son gave me
for Christmas one year from my own CD collection.
He wanted to give me something he knew I'd like
and didn't think I'd notice it was missing.)

Any time my brother gives me lip, I remind him
I swept his leg away at karate class.
We only started because people were trying to bully us –
we weren't from that area.

After 2 weeks I told everybody I was really good,
ask my brother I'd say. *I took him out, easy.*

He's got his own list of favourite movie quotes:
      It's like a finger pointing towards the moon.
      if you concentrate on the finger you miss
      all that heavenly glory.

He's got his own lexicon of jokes:
      Chuck Norris.
      Steven Seagal.

His girlfriend keeps asking him to put away
his trophies and medals because they clutter up the house.

I think Five Star are poor Jackson 5 impersonators
but he insists they're great.
He urges me to check out *Hard Race.*
It's his daily work out / posing in the mirror tune.
He assures me it's a classic.

We share:
      ABC's *Lexicon of Love,*
      McFadden and Whitehead's *Ain't No Stopping Us Now,*
      Trapped by Colonel Abrahams,

a love of old-school conscious hip hop and memories
of climbing the statue of King Alfred on New Years Eve.

He asks people:
      'What have you done to make yourself,
      and the people around you, great today?'

at his Business Studies teaching job and boxercise classes.

Who's the hardest?
I tell him over the phone,
I took you down with a devastating leg sweep.
'If I hadn't held onto you, you'd have fallen flat on the ground.

He laughs,
    'I was 13. You packed in after a month!
    You know I'm a Shotokan black belt 5th Dan now, yeah?
    I've represented Great Britain. I've kicked arses
    all over the world.
    I am legally obliged to warn people my hands
    are deadly weapons -
    except for the mad guy who came at me in the street
    with a Samurai sword.'

My brother:
    can quote line for line, the entire script of
    Enter The Dragon.

He claims
    Chuck Norris is only famous because he got beaten up
    by Bruce Lee in *Way of the Dragon* and he will not
    countenance any discussion on the flamboyant
    yet ineffective skills of Steven Seagal.

He says:
        Belief in God can take you far.
        Belief in the power of a Rabbit's foot
        can have the same effect.

When we meet up the first thing he says is
he's down to his fighting weight.
I tell him that the intricately choreographed Katas, he's been
perfecting for over 30 years, look like bad disco dancing –
then I run.

I love my brother. I
        love him enough to give Five Star another listen.
        I play, listen, repeat.
I'm underwhelmed.
It sounds like tepid soul RnB. I'm unmoved
even by a video version with images of medal-
winning athletes from London 2012 Olympics.

I wonder, is it me?
Were the Pearson family quintet just around
at the wrong time be part of my soundtrack?

After all, my brother is four years younger.
No. That's not it.
I just don't think they are very good.
Why have Five Star when you can have the Jackson 5,
Janet Jackson or Michael Jackson records?

Why have an impersonator when you can listen
to the originals, the real deal?
Aretha and Otis are both great, both individual.

I'll admit my brother is the hardest –
        one of a kind,
        but I have the best music taste.

ALL HAIL THE CHIEF

A displaced, fractured diaspora still need chiefs, tribal elders.

It is my pleasure, my blessing to have known,
to have him be an integral part of my life,
the greatest living being in the history of planet.

This is not a phrase I throw about lightly.

I have wavered many times in my belief in God
but never doubted my belief in my Godfather.

To my young head his only flaw
(and thereby proof that he was human)
is that he didn't advertise his greatness
which is why you've never heard of him.

I called him Uncle John.
He was Dr. John Roberts QC,
first Black Judge (born of African descent) in this country.

Always smiling.
His picture sits proudly on my mother's mantelpiece
resplendent with white wig and medals.

My wife believes I love him more than my own mother.
I say my mother has always been in the top 2.
And she's cool with that.

I rarely saw him when I was younger,
he was busy doing Lawyer things.

When my parents got married
he paid the deposit on their first flat.
When I aced the 11 plus but the council decided
not to send me to the local grammar school,
he tried to intervene.

In my youth, when I was bombarded by negative stereotypes
of black people I knew that they were wrong because
I knew Uncle John:
The real deal. Top lawyer, briefcase, pinstripe suit,
matching tie and pocket handkerchief, disarming smile.

Look up the top 3 lawyers in the world?
    (1) Mandela.
    (2) Ghandi.
    (3) Uncle John.

The International Criminal Court wanted him
to be one of the judges that dealt with UN
backed tribunals into War Crimes.
He holds the Guinness World Record for being a Judge
in the most countries but refused to sanction it.
He said 'It wasn't about him'.

He couldn't have done it without his wife Aunty Eulette.
They were an iconic team.
She said they could never go on holiday because he'd nip
into the local courthouse to see what was going on and
end up working.

Having been in the RAF, he would fly himself
between cases to save time.

He found my long lost elder brother in the Caribbean.
On the weekends he blended in, looked like any other
old black man chilling out.

He wanted to write his autobiography
but never found the time.
He deserves an encyclopaedia to himself and not
my light touch.
When I was younger he said to me:
'Always tell the truth. I will defend you with everything I've got.
But if you break the law, I will drive you to jail myself.'

He had a claret red Rolls Royce
then a claret red walking frame.
I sang songs with him, jammed with him on the guitar
whilst he played hymns on the organ.
He loved a Latin mass on a Sunday.

His firm belief was that everybody should train to be a lawyer.
His grandson remembers him as the one with a sweet
tooth handing out glacier mints.

At his funeral
a choir of white-haired Sierra Leonean school friends
wearing the old school tie sang in Latin in front
of a packed congregation. Letters came from Prime ministers,
leaders, dignitaries from all around the world.

I discovered he had lots of godsons but that didn't diminish
the feeling of being special.

They gave him a CBE.
After all he had done for this country and the world
I thought it was an insult.
He should've been knighted long ago.
He could talk for England, win a debate on any topic.

When he was wheelchair bound and Aunty Eulette was out,
I carried him up the stairs so he could look through his papers.
He said. 'Shhh. Nobody has to know.'
I massaged his feet for hours
when his speech started to go I could still understand
what he was saying. I would massage his head
from the time I arrived in the morning
until the time I left in the evening.

Any tricky situation I ask myself *'What would Uncle John do*?'
The older I get, the more I understand,
it's about the work not the praise.
Making sure the acclaim doesn't get in the way.

He was flawless.
He's in heaven giving the creator some much needed advice.
I don't cry at his passing because I knew
what I had from the very beginning.

There is one lie in this.
I miss him.
I cry all the time.

DUKE ROAD REPRISE

When I went back to Chiswick
for Uncle John's 80th birthday
I had a walk around my old primary school.

Aluminium goal posts.
Street houses, smaller
but the church looked bigger.

Leo enjoyed acting up so much
he became a professional.

Although he's got a Hollywood agent
he spends most of his time fixing up houses.

There is a bad-guy part for him
in every crime story I write

If this gets made into a movie,
he can walk on at the end and play himself.

We can zoom into a frame of us
happily drinking pints in a pub.

Michael, the adopted Chinese
boy from across the road, learnt Mandarin,
tracked down his real parents, moved to the Far East.

Leo can't remember being in Robin Hood
(maybe I remembered it wrong)

'I do remember being thrown out
of the choir for abridging lyrics for "humorous" effect,'
Leo says 'Rather loudly, it turns out. '

If the film of this ever gets made,
the TV actress Judith Jacobs
(from the Real McCoy and EastEnders)
who used to live two doors down on Duke Road,
will play my mum.

THE END

THE LAST WORD

The end?

That's it?

Barely a word about my mum?

The woman who carried me in her belly for nine months,
worked hard, ate the right foods, taught me to read and write,
sewed my clothes, patched up my trousers,
knitted my jumpers, moved her work shifts around to look after
me and my brother, rebuilt her life more times than I care to
remember, dealt in bitcoins before I even knew what they
were, the leader of the Church Mothers' Union, deliverer of so
many NHS babies into the world that she was inundated with
presents every year from grateful mothers.

The woman who is still organising everybody when she should
be putting her feet up, the woman who is still positive when
she is surrounded by an ever-decreasing circle of Caribbean
friends she came to the UK with, to answer the nursing call of
the motherland.

The woman who brought me African food to protect
my strength when I was in hospital. The woman who took
bandanas in for my younger brother to protect his hair when
he was in hospital. The woman who always asks, 'When are
you going to move your records out? You know you don't live
here any more, right?'

The woman who speaks posher than the Queen (which is
where I am sure my daughter gets it from).
The woman who, when she goes on holiday, always brings
me back a t-shirt. (Stop it mum, I'm 51.) The one who plays
the piano and sings in the Church choir, so that's where I get
my musicality from.

The woman who loves The Drifters, Lionel Richie and Whoopi
Goldberg in Sister Act. I forget how many times she's watched
the films and seen the musical. I'm sure those are the
soundtrack to her life.

I keep hassling her to tell her own story but until then, this will
have to do.
The number of words I write about her,
has nothing to do with the level of her impact on my life.
I call her every week.
I may act a little crazy sometimes, even clueless
but I know without her, I wouldn't be here.

ONCE IN A LIFETIME (BONUS TRACK)

I

UEL (University of East London) 1988

I have developed Superpowers.
          I am a shapeshifter.
                              Chameleon.

My Clark Kent glasses,
long black coat and jeans appear
in many forms in any given situation.

                              I am a butterfly.
I flit from event to event, never resting:
          taking the A train with Jazz guitar riffs,
shuffle my way
through Gothic indie shoe-gazing nights –
restricted movements built into the dance formations.

I talk to Northern girls about 'Prefab Sprout'
being the soundtrack to their lives.

I am the butterfly chameleon trapped
in a maze of interconnecting halls - with mirrored walls
                    laced in kryptonite.
I am looking, searching for synergy in the music.

One hit wonders,
'Doctor and the Medics' piss-up their careers in front of me.
No hit wonders,

'The La's' break-down their careers in front of me.
Old glam-rockers nobody remembers,
'The Sweet' detox their careers in front of me.

I talk to Northern girls about 'The Smiths'
being the soundtrack to their lives.

II

I follow the loudest sonic vibrations
through the crumbling Victorian architecture.
All transformers, shapeshifting chameleons,
have an original shape and colour when not trying to adapt.

I walk the corridor, peel off my exterior,
take off my glasses. Sita is on the door:
petite, slim, short cropped black hair, Indian Psychology
major.

She recognises my chest logo, lets me in.
Money not required.

The heaviness of the bass when the doors open
makes my feet vibrate. Everybody's moving to the beat –
        on the one.   Wall-to-wall
multicultural Funkateers,
        jumping, unified, leaping in time.
                Busting moves wearing matching t-shirts.

Why have a Superman 'S' when
you can have a powerful Lion, the Premier club symbol –

and it is Friday night.

Premier Club: formed from the union
of the Afro-Caribbean Society
and the Funk and Fashion Society
to create something all encompassing,
bigger, better, stronger, more dominant, more energizing.

We are lions and lionesses in our Sanctuary
bathed in synchronised red and white lights
          cutting up the darkness. I stretch,
let the funk take over my body –
or am I just letting my soul out of its cage?

I'm not the best dancer, not even in the top 50 –
doesn't matter.
Graham Nelson-Williams, The G.N.W a.k.a Gee One
The latest President, is popping, locking, freezing,
throwing his hips and doing the splits on tables.

Sugar Bear's underground rap hit *Don't Scandalize Mine*
(that samples Talking Heads *Once in a Lifetime*)
is roaring from the speakers.   The MCs point
                and yell out our names.

We are lions and lionesses of the weekend,
and every weekend -
taking over cramped kitchens,
scaffolding, enclosed courtyards, nightclubs, houses.

Wherever we can find space,
plug in the turntables and unleash the sound:

Cheryl Lynn - *Encore*, Blackbyrds - *Rock Creek Park*,
Jackson Sisters – *I Believe in Miracles*,
Salt n Papa - *Push it*,
EPMD, Rob Base and DJ E-Z Rock, Keith Sweat, Guy,
Teddy Riley classics.

I live on a diet of Jollof rice and New Jack Swing.

III

Sunday morning.
I walk,
red amber streetlights under the white sky.
Headphones on,
slow-jams and James Brown remixes fill my ears.

My Clark Kent glasses, long black coat and jeans appear
in many forms in any given situation.

All transformations have a price, a cost of entry.
What if I am reflecting, what I've always been?

Free.

How can I shuffle when I was born to dance?
How can I be flapping fragile wings at 12 times a second
when I can be grooving to high grade funk
at 120 beats per minute?

Monday,
I talk to northern girls about...
the essential Soundtrack to my life.

100

IV

2018?
Still dancing, busting moves,
still living life in the Premier style:
Roaring loud, never silent, always unified
still watching Graham Nelson-Williams a.k.a Gee One –
    the sax-playing funky President,
        chatting on the mic, showing how it's done.
And by the way,
I tell everyone on Mondays through to Sundays,
7 days a week, about the Lion people
and the Premier Club Soundtrack to my life.